First World War
and Army of Occupation
War Diary
France, Belgium and Germany

41 DIVISION
Divisional Troops
Divisional Trench Mortar Batteries
1 March 1918 - 29 October 1918

WO95/2625/6

The Naval & Military Press Ltd
www.nmarchive.com
Published in association with The National Archives

Published by

The Naval & Military Press Ltd

Unit 10 Ridgewood Industrial Park,

Uckfield, East Sussex,

TN22 5QE England

Tel: +44 (0) 1825 749494

www.naval-military-press.com

www.nmarchive.com

This diary has been reprinted in facsimile from the original. Any imperfections are inevitably reproduced and the quality may fall short of modern type and cartographic standards.

© Crown Copyright
Images reproduced by permission of The National Archives, London, England, 2015.

Contents

Document type	Place/Title	Date From	Date To
Heading	WO95/2625/8 41 Div Div Trench Mortar Batt Mar 1918-Oct 1918		
War Diary		01/03/1918	07/03/1918
War Diary	Vedelago	01/03/1918	07/03/1918
War Diary	Doullens Milly Moullens Achiet Le Grand Essarts Souastre F	11/03/1918	31/03/1918
Miscellaneous	The Personnel by this Battery were attached to the 41st D.A.C. during this month		
War Diary	Vedelago	01/03/1918	07/03/1918
War Diary	Treviso	07/03/1918	07/03/1918
War Diary	Doullens	11/03/1918	31/03/1918
Heading	41st Divisional Artillery D.T.M.O. & X.Y.Z. Trench Mortars April 1918		
Miscellaneous	The Battery did not function this month. Officers this were otherwise employed by D.A.		
War Diary	Souastre	01/04/1918	30/04/1918
Miscellaneous	Casualties		
War Diary	Souastre	01/04/1918	30/04/1918
War Diary	Souastre	26/04/1918	26/04/1918
War Diary	Henu	01/05/1918	06/05/1918
War Diary	Gommecourt	06/05/1918	06/05/1918
War Diary	Bayencourt	06/05/1918	06/05/1918
War Diary	Henu	11/05/1918	11/05/1918
War Diary	Pas	12/05/1918	13/05/1918
War Diary	Doullens	14/05/1918	14/05/1918
War Diary	Waayenburgh	15/05/1918	15/05/1918
War Diary	Ypres	16/05/1918	05/06/1918
War Diary	Bambecque	06/06/1918	06/06/1918
War Diary	Zeggers-Cappel	07/06/1918	07/06/1918
War Diary	Ruminghem	08/06/1918	08/06/1918
War Diary	Leulinghem	11/06/1918	28/06/1918
War Diary	Watou-France	29/06/1918	30/06/1918
War Diary	Scherpenberg La Clytte Sector	01/07/1918	31/07/1918
War Diary	(Hooggraaf) 28/A.32.a.	01/08/1918	01/08/1918
War Diary	Scherpenberg La Clytte Sector	01/08/1918	31/08/1918
War Diary		21/08/1918	31/08/1918
War Diary	Hoograff	01/09/1918	05/09/1918
War Diary	La Clytte	06/09/1918	07/09/1918
War Diary	Ouderdom.	08/09/1918	10/09/1918
War Diary	Woesten.	20/09/1918	30/09/1918
War Diary	Dickebusch	01/10/1918	02/10/1918
War Diary	Near Geluwe.	05/10/1918	05/10/1918
War Diary	Geluvelt	05/10/1918	16/10/1918
War Diary	Moorseele	17/10/1918	20/10/1918
War Diary	Courtrai	21/10/1918	22/10/1918
War Diary	Hooghe	25/10/1918	25/10/1918
War Diary	Courtrai	27/10/1918	29/10/1918

WO 95/2625/8
41 DIV
DIV TRENCH MORTAR BATT
MAR 1918 - OCT 1918

WAR DIARY
INTELLIGENCE SUMMARY

X/41 T.M.B.   MARCH 1918

Army Form C. 2118

Place	Date	Hour	Summary of Events and Information	Remarks and references to Appendices
	1st to 6th		The battery was lent to the D.T.M.O 5th Div. for operations. Battery proceeded to France with the 41st DAC and did not function for the remainder of the month. Men were employed under orders of DAC.	

A.S.P Shea, Lt RFA

OC 4/41

WAR DIARY
INTELLIGENCE SUMMARY

MARCH 1918 Y/41 T.M.B. Army Form C. 2118.

(Erase heading not required.)

Place	Date	Hour	Summary of Events and Information	Remarks and references to Appendices
	MCH			
VEDELAGO	1-7		THIS BATTERY WAS ATTACHED TO 41st D.A.C FOR FATIGUES ETC	
	7		ENTRAINED FOR FRANCE	
DOULLENS MILLY MOULLENS ACHIEF LE-GRAND ESSARTS SOUASTRE	11 – 31		THIS BATTERY WAS ATTACHED TO 41 D.A.C FOR FATIGUES. ETC.	

March 31/1918

R B Renwick Capt R.F.A.
O/c Y/41 T.M.B.

WAR DIARY
or
INTELLIGENCE SUMMARY
(Erase heading not required.)

Army Form C. 2118

MARCH 1918

Z/41 T.M.B.

Place	Date	Hour	Summary of Events and Information	Remarks and references to Appendices
			The personnel of this Battery were attached to the 41st D.A.C. during this month.	
			Casualties:— Nil	
			A. Fuller Lt. R.F.A. O.C. Z/41 T.M.B.	

WAR DIARY

INTELLIGENCE SUMMARY

(Erase heading not required.)

Army Form C. 2118

MARCH 1918

HEADQUARTERS 41 T.M.B's.

Instructions regarding War Diaries and Intelligence Summaries are contained in F.S. Regs., Part II. and the Staff Manual respectively. Title Pages will be prepared in manuscript.

Place	Date	Hour	Summary of Events and Information	Remarks and references to Appendices
	MCH			VK 25
VEDELAGO	1-7		HEADQUARTERS 41 T M B's.	
TREVISO	7		ENTRAINED FOR FRANCE	
DOULLENS	11		DETRAINED	
	11-31		ATTACHED TO 41 D.A.C	

H.Q. TRENCH MORTAR BATTERIES, 41st DIVISION.
No.............
Date 31/3/18

A.E. Cundall Capt. R.T.A.
1 D.T.M.O. 41 Division

41st Divisional Artillery

D.T.M.O. & X.Y.Z. TRENCH MORTARS

APRIL 1918

… APRIL 1918

X/41 T.M.B.

WAR DIARY or INTELLIGENCE SUMMARY

Army Form C. 2118

The Battery did not function this month. Officers & men were otherwise employed by D.A.

A.S. Renshaw
Lt. R.F.A
o/c X/41 T.M.B.

WAR DIARY or INTELLIGENCE SUMMARY

Y/41 T.M.B.

APRIL 1918

Army Form C. 2118

Place	Date	Hour	Summary of Events and Information	Remarks and references to Appendices
SOUASTRE Etc	Apl 1-30		This Battery was attached to 41 D.A.C for fatigues Etc	

April 30/1918.

RG Burnett Capt. R.F.A.
O/c Y/41 T.M.B.

WAR DIARY

or

INTELLIGENCE SUMMARY Z/41 T.M.B

(Erase heading not required.)

APRIL 1918

Army Form C. 2118

Instructions regarding War Diaries and Intelligence Summaries are contained in F.S. Regs., Part II. and the Staff Manual respectively. Title Pages will be prepared in manuscript.

Place	Date	Hour	Summary of Events and Information	Remarks and references to Appendices
			The personnel of the Battery were attached to 5th H. D.A.C. until the 25 inst that and that Battery was disbanded owing to re-organization of T.M. batteries. Casualties :— Nil A. Fallen R.F.A. 2/Lt. T.M.B	

Army Form C. 2118

WAR DIARY
or
INTELLIGENCE SUMMARY
(Erase heading not required.)

HEADQUARTERS 41 T.M.B's

APRIL 1918

Place	Date	Hour	Summary of Events and Information	Remarks and references to Appendices
SOMASTRE	Apl. 1-30		Headquarters 41 T.M.B's attached to 41 D.A.C.	M 26
	Apl. 26		Batteries re-organised. Personnel of Z/41 T.M.B absorbed in X/41 & Y/41 T.M.B's	

H.Q. Trench Mortar Batteries, 41st Division.
No. ....
Date 30/4/18

J.E. Blundell Capt. RFA
D.T.M.O
41 Division.

Army Form C. 2118.

WAR DIARY
or
INTELLIGENCE SUMMARY.
(Erase heading not required.)

R.A. HEADQUARTERS
#1 TRENCH MORTAR BATTERIES R.A.
Vol 2

Place	Date	Hour	Summary of Events and Information	Remarks and references to Appendices
HENU.	1st MAY – 6th MAY		Personnel of T.M. Batteries attached 41st DTMC.	SCRA
COMMECOURT	6th MAY		X/41 relieved 7/42 in the line at COMMECOURT.	SCRA
BAYENCOURT	"		7/41 went into billets at BAYENCOURT.	SCRA
HENU.	11th		Capt E.C.R. HADDOW reported for duty as D.T.M.O. (posted from 59th D.A.)	SCRA
PAS.	12th		X/41 relieved by X/57. Both batteries withdrew to BOIS ST PIERRE PAS.	SCRA
"	12th		18 O.R. posted to the Bde. from 59th Divn. T.M's.	SCRA
DOULLENS	14		Batteries entrained at DOULLENS. To personnel 5 YPRES front.	SCRA
WAAYENBURGH	15		Batteries detrained at WAAYENBURGH 9.30 am – proceeded to camp at HAMHOEK.	SCRA
YPRES	16		Y/41 relieved 7/29 in the line. Six 6" T.M's in defensive positions taken over.	SCRA
"	18		Rest billets camp moved to RYDE CAMP.	SCRA
"	18th to 31st		4 forward positions built for 6" T.M's to relieve Sigs. Bno in ECOLE for R.A. Bde. front & two in POTISZE Rd for Lyth Bde. front.	R.P.A.
"	"		4 Reserve positions built for defence of BRIELEN LINE – these positions just to the	R.P.A.
"	19th		EAST of GOLDFISH CHAU. Personnel to Cdg Base DTMC to follow 187th Bde. 14. – 19th Bde. 14. – S.A.C.	CURH
"			12.	

2353 Wt. W2544/1454 700,000 5/15 D. D. & L. A.D.S.S./Forms/C. 2118.

Army Form C. 2118.

WAR DIARY
INTELLIGENCE SUMMARY
(Erase heading not required.)

Place	Date	Hour	Summary of Events and Information	Remarks and references to Appendices
YPRES.	MAY 26th		3 - 6" T.M's complete received from TADOS 4th Bn. Lieut A.W. PEWTRESS + 2 OR. to ANTI-GAS Course at II Corps School.	SCRA SCRA
	31st		2 - 6" T.M's complete received from TADOS 4th Bn.	SCRA
			Strength 1st May 1918. 10 OFF. 84. OR.	SCRA
			" 31st May 1918. 11 " 111 OR	SCRA
			Battle casualties during the month. 6 wounded (gas) [1 since died].	SCRA

Edgar Shannon Capt RFA
D.T.M.O. 4th Bn. 8th Div.

WAR DIARY
INTELLIGENCE SUMMARY

Trench Mortar Batteries 41 Div

JUNE 1918

Army Form. C. 2118

Vol 28

Place	Date	Hour	Summary of Events and Information	Remarks and references to Appendices
YPRES	1st to 4th		4th T.M. Batteries in action in YPRES.	SCRA
"	5th		41st T.M. Batteries relieved by 49th Divl. T.M. Batteries.	SCRA
BAMBECQUE	6th		41st T.M. Batteries moved by lorry to BAMBECQUE AREA.	SCRA
ZEGGERS-CAPPEL	7th		" " " " to ZEGGERS-CAPPEL AREA	SCRA
RUMINGHEM	8th		" " " " to RUMINGHEM	SCRA
			Party of 48 O.R. sent to Calais on Removal party.	
LEDLINGHEM	11th to 28th		41st T.M. Batteries attached to II Army T.M. School for training.	SCRA
WATOU, FRANCE	29th		41st T.M. Batteries moved by lorry to WATOU, FRANCE & commence work in accommodation for	SCRA
	30th		Party of 75 O.R. sent into the line to T.M. position. 30 O.R. attached to 187th Essex R.F.A. for temporary duty. 187th T.M. position.	SCRA

Signed. Sharples Capt RFA
4th T.M.O.
2/7/18

19-9.

JULY TO SEPT 741

WAR DIARY
INTELLIGENCE SUMMARY
(Erase heading not required.)

Army Form C. 2118

41st T.M. BATTERIES R.A.

VOL 27

Instructions regarding War Diaries and Intelligence Summaries are contained in F.S. Regs., Part II. and the Staff Manual respectively. Title Pages will be prepared in manuscript.

Place	Date	Hour	Summary of Events and Information	Remarks and references to Appendices
WATOU - FRANCE		8.0pm	41st Trench Mortar Batteries R.A. moved from WATOU - FRANCE Strength of unit 9 officers 81 O.R. (1400 GC RAAF (2)(Q.32.a)) to cover the front	ECRA
SCHERPENBERG - LA CLYTTE SECTOR	1st to 31st		During the month a band Mortar emplacements were constructed on line system to cover the SCHERPENBERG - DICKE BUSCH LAKE line. Reporting T.M. personnel with 22 men of 41st Dir. attached was engaged in preparing i.e. Cable buried trench on Artillery OR with hurdles.	ECRA ECRA ECRA
" "	31st		Casualties 1 O.R. Keene. Strength of unit 9 officers 104 O.R.	

Major Hadow Capt RFA
I.T.M.O. 41st Div. Arty.

H.Q. TRENCH MORTAR BATTERIES, 41st DIVISION.

AUGUST 1918

Army Form C. 2118.

WAR DIARY
or
INTELLIGENCE SUMMARY. Trench Mortar Batteries R.A. 41 Division
(Erase heading not required.)

Vol 28

Place	Date	Hour	Summary of Events and Information	Remarks and references to Appendices
(HOOGGRAAF) 28/A.32.a	1st	—	41 Divl. T.M. Batteries remained at Billet in this neighbourhood. Strength of Unit: 9 Officers, 104 O.R.	
SCHERPENBERG — LA CLYTTE Sector	1st to 31st		T.M. Personnel engaged exclusively in manning 10 6" T.M. positions built in preceding month. These mortars manned day & night on S.O.S. lines. Four forward mortars registered as follows:— 2 Wedgwood Guns — Aug. 5. 53 rounds. 2 Jeremy 7m Guns — Aug. 10. 13 rounds. There was a Short form No.1 of Wedgwood Guns on Aug. 8. when 36 rounds were fired in preparation for Raid.	
	31st		On the enemy withdrawing from Mt. Kemmel, the manning of all positions ceased & personnel returned to billet to rest.	
	21st		Moved to new farm at L.29.B.5.1. (Sheet 28). Casualties during month: 1 O.R. wounded. Rounds expended during month: 104. All shooting was done by 1/41 2M.B.	
	31st		Strength of Unit at end of month: 9 Officers, 101 O.R.	

O. Riley, Capt. R.F.A.
9 D.T.M.O. /41 Div.
1/9/18.

SEPTEMBER 1918. Army Form C. 2118.

WAR DIARY
or
INTELLIGENCE SUMMARY. Trench Mortar Batteries, R.A. 41st Division
(Erase heading not required.)

Place	Date	Hour	Summary of Events and Information	Remarks and references to Appendices
HOOGRAAF	1st		Personnel of X/41 & Y/41 M.T.M. Btys. engaged on fatigues & withdrawing Trench Mortars from positions on SCHERPENBERG – DICKEBUSCH LAKE line.	L.P.A.
	2nd			L.P.A.
LA CLYTTE	6 & 7th		Exchange of 8 four guns after enemy's withdrawal.	L.P.A.
OUDERDOM	8th		41st T.M. Batteries relieved by 34th T.M. Batteries. No guns or stores exchanged.	L.P.A.
"	9th		Personnel engaged on fatigues with the Artillery Brigades – training them on composition – Ammunition dumps.	L.P.A.
	19th			
"	10th		Two Officers and 8 O.R. to 6" T.M. Course at Army T.M. School.	L.P.A.
WOESTEN	20th		X/41 T.M. Batteries moved to WOESTEN area attached to 6th Belgian Infantry Division.	L.P.A.
	21st			L.P.A.
	27th		12 6" T.M's put in action at FRANCOIS FARM & VON VERDEN HOUSE. 75 rounds of ammunition per gun	
	28th		Y/41 & X/41 took positions. 3 hour bombardment of enemy's forward posts. 860 rounds ammunition expended.	L.P.A.
	30th		Personnel & guns withdrew to ELVERDINGHE. Barrage fire for Reinaert Ridge. Killed 1 Officer, Wounded 1 Officer 2 O.R.	L.P.A.

Tym Stadaunt, Capt. R.T.A.
D.T.M.O. 41st D.A.

1/10 /18.

Army Form C. 2118.

OCTOBER 1918 WAR DIARY T.M. Batteries
INTELLIGENCE SUMMARY 41st DIVLN. ARTY

Vol 32

Place	Date	Hour	Summary of Events and Information	Remarks and references to Appendices
DICKEBUSCH	1 & 2	—	Personnel of T.M. Batteries sent to Arty. Base & Battle.	ERA
NEAR GELUWE	5th		Personalized positions for 4 6' T.M's near GILLOW FARM.	ERA
GELUVELT	"		Personnel collected together at GELUVELT, ready to commence building T.M. positions.	ERA
	6th		Building T.M. positions. 4 guns in action. Firing commenced.	ERA
"	9th			
"	10th		Two guns & 200 rounds ammunition flown up.	ERA
"	11th		Two new T.M. positions chosen. Work commenced	ERA
"	13th		Firing finished & personnel withdrawn from the line to "huts" at GELUVELT.	ERA
	16th		1 Officer sent to OATHS to draw remounts.	ERA
MOORSEELE	17th		T.M. Batteries moved with No 2 Sectn SFA to MOORSEELE	ERA
	19th		Remainder of guns & stores together with four mule carriages brought up to MOORSEELE from DICKEBUSCH	ERA
	20th		Two fatigue parties supplied for drawing remounts	ERA
COURTRAI	21st		T.M. Batteries move to outskirts of COURTRAI (near MARCKE)	ERA
	"			ERA

OCTOBER 1918 WAR DIARY T.M. BATTERIES
INTELLIGENCE SUMMARY 41st DIVN. ARTY

Army Form C. 2118.

Place	Date	Hour	Summary of Events and Information	Remarks and references to Appendices
COURTRAI.	22		2/Lt J.E. HOCRAFT & 2/Lt posted to 190 Bde RFA	SIGN
HOOGHE	25.		2/Lt E.C. HENTY & 2/Lt LEDBURY joined as reinforcement officers.	SIGN
			T.M. Batteries moved to HOOGHE.	
COURTRAI	27		T.M. Batteries moved to COURTRAI.	SIGN
	28		2 Officers & 7 O.R. to Army T.M. School	SIGN
	29		Personnel to Bde. & DTMO	SIGN
			Strength of Batteries 1st Oct. 8 OFF. 105 O.R.	SIGN
			" 31st " 9 " 99 "	SIGN
			Casualties. — NIL —	SIGN

Sgd. Blandow Capt RFA
D.T.M.O. 41st Divl. Arty.

www.ingramcontent.com/pod-product-compliance
Lightning Source LLC
Chambersburg PA
CBHW081252170426
43191CB00037B/2135